Contents

Acknowledgments

We would like to acknowledge our family, friends and the customers that we have encountered over the years that have become friends. With all of your support we have been able to thrive beyond what we could of ever think or imagine. In addition to the support, the love has been unforgettable and we appreciate it. The Prayer Closet Resale Shop realizes that all of you mentioned were a part of the plan to bring the vision into existence, and for that, we thank you!

Introduction

Before, I met my husband, I was a single mother raising a son, he was a senior in high school at the time and I was in between jobs working temporary assignments. After my son graduated from high school, my financial status changed. One of the biggest challenges I experienced was that I barely had enough money to shop for clothing, after paying the household expenses. How quickly I realized that shopping for clothes was something that I've always taken for granted. Who actually says to themselves it's going to come a day when I can't buy a new outfit or a new pair of shoes? Not too many people that you know of right?

Needless to say, I prayed to God constantly about how I can make ends meet and continue to be able to shop every now and then. One day, I went into a thrift store looking for a piece of furniture. This particular store I went into they also sold clothing. I browsed around at the clothing and shoes and I have to admit, shopping at a thrift store wasn't high on my priority list or my first choice. My trip to this particular thrift store was the beginning for me on how I prefer to shop for clothing, shoes and accessories. The thrill of finding something that nobody else had was great! Truth be told, how many of you know that when you go out and see someone with the same outfit on that you have on, your confidence gets a little stirred up?

That little voice in our head starts speaking to us saying, "I look better or I like the way that outfit looks on them" (Smile).

Shortly after I started shopping at thrift and consignments stores, I noticed that their store prices were becoming outrageous. The prices were starting to look more like the retail prices. This wasn't looking good to me. My first thought was, what are they doing, something has to be done about this. After complaining to family members and friends and driving around town in search of a cheaper thrift stores, I realized that I was wasting gas and opinions. Sure I kept on shopping at the stores but it wasn't as frequent.

My experience in seeing the increased prices at some thrift and resale stores was what propelled me to branch out and open up The Prayer Closet Resale Shop. I've always wanted to open up a store but never in my wildest dreams did I think that God would lead me in this direction for this type of store. When the vision first came to me back in 2005, I envisioned opening up a Christian bookstore. As you can see God's plans are not like our plans. Since I have followed the plan which was contrary to my plan, the Prayer Closet has been a blessing to my family and the communities we have been able to serve.

So with the experiences that I and the business have gone through since this journey, we were compelled to share and encourage others how to overcome challenges.

This book will give you tips on how to shop for less and what to look for when shopping at thrift stores. After you read this book you will never shop the same way again. Let's begin shall we?

Chapter One

How to Put Together Five Different Looks

This wardrobe combination is so simple and unique that we overlook it. After doing a survey of my closet I came across five outfits that didn't cost me a dime. I had a couple of pant suits and skirt suits that I have always wore together whenever I went on an interview for a job. On this one particular day while I was in the process of grabbing my navy skirt suit, a light bulb went off. Instead of wearing the skirt to the suit, I paired the skirt with a taupe colored jacket, along with a cream colored shell top. My jewelry was gold and my shoes were the same color as the jacket.

The second time I went on an interview I pulled out my gray pantsuit and swapped out the pieces again. This outfit consisted in wearing the gray blazer with a black pair of pants. My blouse was white zebra print which tied into a bow at the neck, I pinned a black flower on my lapel which drew the attention away from my gray jacket. My shoes were black patent leather platform pumps. The flower made a bold jewelry piece along with some black earrings which didn't over power the flowered pin attached to my lapel.

You can pair bright colors with your basic navy, black, white or cream colored bottoms or tops for a different look. Oftentimes at my store I dress the mannequins in bold colors which I like to call the attention grabber.

Customers come in like clockwork buying the outfits right off of the mannequins! Most of the customers never thought to mix pieces the way I have done and do on the mannequins. If you don't have any bright colored tops or bottoms, mix up your colors with some bold colorful jewelry.

The human eye is trained to zoom in on colors and then our eyes will go up and down or from side to side. On the following page I inserted a few photos of some outfits I mixed up or added bold accessories to give you an idea on how to create different outfits.

Black pinstriped skirt &
powder blue jacket

Black Sheath Dress &
Linen Shirt worn as a jacket

The third outfit can consist of wearing a pinstriped blazer as a coat in the fall with a nice scarf and a pair of jeans with platform pumps or boots. A nice shell can be worn with the jeans and a bright orange or red ruffled scarf draped around your neck. This outfit is good for wearing to your children or grandchildren's little league football games or high school football games.

The fourth outfit I have paired together are cool summer outfits which you will see the photos on the next page. In one of the photos you will see a brown sundress paired with a pair of capri leggings. This is a cool outfit to have fun in. If you have a dress that has shrunk for some apparent reason get creative and put on a pair of capri's or leggings underneath it. The fifth outfit is a pair of white gauchos which are paired with a cute blue and white striped top. On the 4th of July I added red accessories to the blue and white outfit on the next page which was a hit.

The trick is to use what you already have to create a new look. If you do not have the basic colors in your wardrobe shop at Goodwill or thrift stores that have half off of the colored ticket item for that day.

These outfits you will see below were fun to mix and match up. I've had some customers come into our store and ask for my assistance on picking out their wardrobes. As women get older we are discovering that incorporating color into our wardrobes brings about youthfulness and a glow.

Ladies these tips not only apply to you they also apply to our men. You can mix-up their business attire and casual wear as well. For instance, a pair of khaki slacks and a nice colored polo style shirt is good for a casual day at work or for an interview the khaki slacks can be worn with a matching khaki jacket depending on what type of position they are interviewing for.

Sundress and black Capri's   *White gaucho's and cowl top*

Tip:

Be bold and get creative with your wardrobe.

Chapter Two

Set a Budget for Your Shopping Spree

When shopping at thrift stores keep in mind that you should set a budget. As I mentioned in Chapter One, most of these thrift stores have increased their prices tremendously. A year ago you could purchase a woman's suit sold in Goodwill under $10.00 dollars. Although, the suits sold at that price, the sizes didn't match. Example, a Larry Levine pantsuit the jacket is a size 12 and the pants are a size 10 or vice versa. Now when you go into the Goodwill Store you will find a designer suit that costs $20.00 to $25.00 dollars.

When shopping in your big name thrift stores like Salvation Army, Goodwill or Big Value Outlet keep an eye out for the colored ticket items selling at half off. Shopping at your local thrift stores they have some awesome deals on items as low as .25 cents. If you can spend .25 cents and purchase over 7 to 8 outfits under $20.00 dollars wouldn't you rather do that?

Most of you reading this book may already be aware that children's clothing and shoes are much cheaper. In my store our children's clothing prices start from $1.00 up to $4.00 dollars for infants up to 18 months. Beginning at 24 months up to 4T our prices start at $2.00 up to $5.00 dollars.

Another incentive for shopping at your local thrift stores with these types of prices is that these are the best stores to shop at for back to school, summer clothing and Christmas. We do really well on Mother's Day and the high school proms. Most of our women's suits are donated in excellent condition and we sell the suits for $15.00 and $17.00 dollars with a huge savings of $5.00 to $7.00 dollars when you purchase accessories to go along with the Mother's Day and the high school prom dresses.

Tip:

Always set a budget and shop smart.

Dress & Jacket Combo

Shirt & Skirt Combo

2pc Skirt Suit

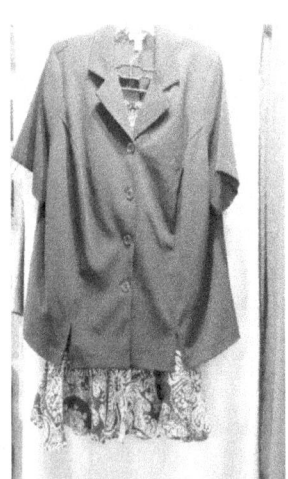

2 pc Skirt Suit

Chapter Three

Where to Shop for Less

When shopping for clothing it's been my experience to shop at some of your smaller thrift and consignment shops first. This is my personal preference to shop this way because some of these smaller business owners aren't trying to compete with the big name thrift and consignment stores. Also, the smaller businesses have unbelievable prices which are great for someone trying to get back out into the workforce or just want a new wardrobe.

As I mentioned in the previous chapter, your number one goal should be setting a budget. Go where your money will take you further. The smaller stores are putting you the consumers needs first. They understand that in this day and age the economy is slowly but surely turning around and that people need to be mindful of their spending habits.

When I opened up my business it was birthed from a need not out of greed. What I mean by this is based on my personal experiences; I realized like me that there are others who feel or felt the same way about the price increase at some of the big named thrift and consignment stores. Consumers turn to thrift and consignment stores for great bargains, one of a kind items, and affordable prices.

Our store has kept this in mind and this is one of the reasons that we're a sought after business today. If we would have jumped on the bandwagon and increased our prices trying to keep up with the big named thrift stores, I wouldn't be here today writing this book and sharing with you these valuable shopping tips.

Now that you know where to shop, and your budget is in place, do you know what you are looking for? It is easy to go into a store and after seeing the low prices you can become excited and splurge. Trust me, I have done this on several occasions, I'm a true witness that this will happen to you one way or another and if it does happen, shake it off and bask in the moment. Here's a visual of what I'm talking about splurging. Example, you will see those perfect shoes that are sitting on the shelf calling your name, you can't be rude and ignore the shoes right, so now you have to purchase them (smile)

Getting back on track of knowing where to shop and why it's beneficial to you and your finances. When shopping at the smaller thrift and consignment stores the business owners is relatable to you (the Customer) needs and wants. Not all of the smaller store owners have this type of compassion but most of them do. It's my belief if you have compassion towards customers; this makes repeat customers and referrals. Compassion is one of the first things I look for when I walk into a thrift or consignment store.

Indications for me that the store lacks compassion is when I enter a store and not feel welcomed, this also says to me that this store does not want my business and they are only concerned about making a sell.

A lot of my customers come back to me and send referrals because of the compassion that we present when they enter into our store. We take pride in our store appearance, the customer needs and wants. Each customer that enters into The Prayer Closet Resale Shop has become friends and a repeat customer. If you ever establish this type of relationship in a thrift store in your area, you have found a new home to shop long after you get back on the financial recovery track.

There are several things to look for when shopping at a smaller thrift and consignment store. Some of the things I look for are the prices, quality and condition of the clothing or furniture, artwork etc. When all of these things suits me this is an indication that I have found a store to shop at regularly. Maybe you have other things in mind when shopping for the right store that are important to you.

Whatever, the indications are for you, keep those in mind while shopping, and continuously ask yourself does this store give me what I'm looking for? Also, remember the purpose of you shopping at thrift and consignment stores is to save money.

Tip:

Shop smart and save money while doing it

Chapter Four

Coordinating and Utilizing Your Purchases

Now that you have made your purchases here are some tips on how to wear and/or use them to work for your purpose. The different scenarios I give you have helped me and in return I have been able to pass these same tips onto my customers, family members and friends.

Scenario One: Business

Ladies if you do not have a nice two piece skirt suit or pant suit, a solid colored blouse and skirt will work for you. Make sure that the skirt is a dark color preferably navy or black. Your shoes and hosiery should be a solid color as well; this shows the interviewer that you are professional. Save the bright colored blouses and open toed shoes after you have landed the job.

Scenario Two: Business Casual

Ladies if you are interviewing for a position in sales, a solid colored blouse with pants is suitable business casual attire. The pant options can be khaki, dark brown, black or gray. Keep it simple with neutral colors. Wearing a flat dressy shoe is suitable preferably a solid color again save the open toe and bright colored shoes after you have landed the job.

Retail jobs may allow you to wear a sneaker type shoe but again, use your discretion and wear appropriate shoe wear for the company you are interviewing with.

Scenario Three: Men's Business

Men are automatically professional when it comes to business attire for an interview. They get it and I have to give them kudos on this trait. This tip is for the young men looking to enter into the workforce. A nice pair of dark colored slacks with a button down long sleeved shirt and tie is presentable. Wear a belt even if the pants fit, this is so important. Your shoes should be a dark color and polished up nicely. Your shoes make a bold statement and will land you the job.

Scenario Two: Business Casual

Men who are interested in positions working in sales their attire can include khaki pants, a nice button down shirt tucked in with a nice leather belt. You can wear a tie or go without one; this is totally up to you. My suggestion is to get a little history about the company first then make your decision if you should wear a tie or not. The shoes can be a nice casual loafer type and save the colored socks, believe it or not you will not be taken seriously by wearing fun socks to an interview. Again, save the fun socks and boat sneakers after you have landed the job.

These scenarios that I have given are to help those who are looking to re-enter into the workforce. Of course, you will have to make the final decision on what you think you should wear or not wear to an interview. Another, thing I highly recommend is getting your clothing ready the day before the interview. This allows you enough time to wash your purchased items from the thrift and consignment stores. Oftentimes, you will not be able to see how the outfit looks on in full view so this is why it's important to get your clothing ready the day before.

For those of you have family that you will be buying for it's important to allow yourself enough time to wash and/or clean your purchases before wearing. At most of the thrift and consignment stores clothes, shoes and accessories are donations. The person or people who donated to these stores may or may not have cleaned the clothing and items, that's why it's always good to rewash your purchases again when you get home.

Tip:

Dress to be successful when interviewing

Chapter Five

Thrifty Shopping for Children

When looking for clothing, shoes, and/or accessories for children and you are on a budget, your first thought should be checking out a thrift or consignment store. Most of their infant and children's clothing is brand new or in very good condition. There are some well known children thrift stores you can check out in your area such as Once Upon A Child and The Children's Place. Once Upon A Child also sell baby furniture (i.e. car seats, high-chairs, cribs, play pens, etc), all at affordable prices. Please check your local area for these two stores mentioned, you will not be disappointed.

Another benefit about Once Upon a Child is that you can sell them your children's clothing, shoes, etc. What you need to know before selling your clothing to them is to make sure that you are bringing clothing that's in season. For example, a winter outfit will not sell in the summer and vice versa. Of course, when selling your clothing, make sure that the clothing and items are in good condition, you will get top dollar for your items which are a plus. Personally I find that children thrift stores are the best places to shop for your children because the people who have donated or sold their clothing to these stores have taken good care of the items.

Of course, please remember to wash the clothing or items before wearing or using because some of the clothing has been washed in a detergent which could cause your child to get an allergic reaction to. For the new items I wouldn't worry too much but it doesn't hurt to rewash the clothing before wearing to be safe. If you are purchasing furniture again, wipe the furniture and toys down.

The types of clothing you can expect to see when you shop at these thrift and consignment stores for children are good quality clothing. Just to give you an idea on what you can expect, I have included some photos of the pieces I have sold at my store on the next page.

Tip:

Keep in mind all items are non refundable

Girls Dress $1.00

Girls Sandals $2.00

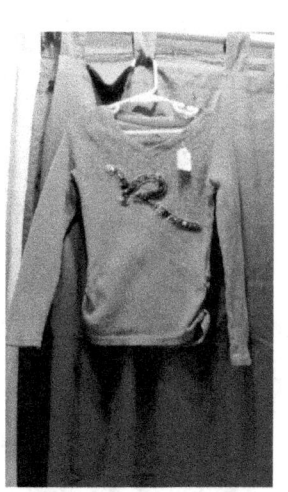

Girls Shirt $3.00

Boys Jeans $4.00

Chapter Six

Why Shopping Thrifty is Smart

The first and second reason why it's smart to shop thrifty is because it's affordable and it's by choice. Regardless of your financial situation thrift shopping is the preferred method of shopping for most consumers. Have you taken a look around your city or town and checked out how many thrift and consignment stores are in your area? Take a minute now and think about it, as a matter of fact, Google how many thrift and consignment stores are in your area. You will agree that thrift shopping is the preferred method for most consumers. Here's something that has occurred to me a while back. A person can go into a thrift store and find something that will catch their eye, they may not purchase it right then, but it's a guarantee that people will see something that catches their eye.

For the antique furniture shoppers whose passion is in restoring old furniture or switch out the cushions or covering on your kitchen or dining room chairs. Here's a tip for you that some of you probably never thought of. The next time you are in a thrift store locate the plus size section and purchase a couple of skirts or shirts. These skirts or shirts can be used as fabric to recover the cushions on an ottoman or a side chair.

You may not find two or more of the same skirts or shirts but you can get something with the same color as your current piece which will compliment the other pieces of furniture you want to recover.

There are so many reasons why you should shop thrifty. Here's one of my favorite reasons is geared more so for the person who likes to sew but can't afford fabric. The next time you shop at a thrift store head to the section where the store sell drapes or fabric shower curtains and reuse as fabric. It's not expensive and the most you could pay for some drapes or shower curtains is .50 to .99 cents. Now how's that for being shopping smart! The best thing about purchases like this is you will not find anyone else with that same fabric walking around anywhere else.

Oftentimes I recycle fabric from my store and use for my personal use. I love to sew and I'm always looking for ways to recycle which makes sense for a resale shop owner right (smile). There was a dress that was donated to our store a few years ago which didn't sell. The dress was a plus size dress. Well being in the business that I am in, I started looking for ways to get this dress sold. After a lot of thought, I decided to alter the dress and make something for myself. The look I created was a 2pc skirt set.

I will close out this chapter by saying; if you like to sew remember to utilize other alternatives when looking for fabric. This saves money in the long run even if you need to save or not.

Tip:

One person's junk is another person's treasure

Chapter Seven

Turning Furniture from Trash to Treasure

This chapter is one of my favorites because of the tips I have learned from others which has allowed me to be creative with my own creations. When you hear the word trash immediately our thought process says broken, old and no longer works. The word treasure is an indication of something dear and worthy to you and I. Did you realize that Americans toss out worthy treasures every year, in addition to throwing away money? I'm going to talk to you about how to change your mindset and recycle those dollars back into your wallet and household.

When looking for affordable furniture the best places to shop in my opinion is at secondhand stores, yard sales and/or estate sales. Again, this is my personal opinion and preference. Are you aware that there are several secondhand stores in addition to yard sales and/or estate sales in your local area occurring every weekend? Before starting a project, I challenge you to check out your local listings in the classifieds for auctions, estate sales, and/or yard sales. Below I'm going to give you a few tips on how to turn your trash to treasure.

Scenario One: Coffee Tables

Search for a coffee table or side table that has a lot of scratches and dings in it from wear and tear. Sand the coffee table or side table and then stain it with a cherry wood stain or maple wood stain. If you're looking for side tables that are not a match but they are a similar shape as the coffee table (i.e. round, rectangle, square) these are great finds. The trick is to make sure the colors of the pieces you have purchased match.

Scenario Two: Kitchen and Dining Table

When recycling wooden kitchen tables sand the table first, and then stain to your color of choice. If the chairs have cushions you can recover the cushions or purchase new chairs. If you can't find a set of 4 or more of the same chairs, you can purchase chairs from another set making sure that the shape of the chairs match (i.e. square, rectangle).

Scenario Three: Floating Shelves

If you have limited kitchen cabinet space and you want to show off some of your fine china, search for a bookshelf with 4 or more shelves and utilize the shelves to show off your dishes. Again you can sand down these shelves and re-stain them to your color of choice.

For plate holders, you can make your own by using wired hangers and bend them into the shape you want. Here's a visual of using wired hangers. Make a "w" shape, cut off the extra hanger and spray paint the hangers black. Voila you have a masterpiece for others to admire.

Scenario Four: Night Stands

Here are some fun ideas that you can use your creativity beyond measure. Hunt for antique end tables as use these as night stands. Spray painting the tables white makes them look like night stands. A good friend of mine created a masterpiece with this particular project. She stenciled butterflies to complete the project. After you created your artwork, spray down the tables with some shellac to seal the paint job.

Scenario Five: Headboard(s)

There are unlimited possibilities here to make headboards. Search for wall mirrors and remove the frames. If you have 3 of the wall mirrors this works and looks better as a headboard. Put the mirrors on the wall horizontally one under another with no gap in between and secure the mirrors with the clear mirror hooks. If you are really crafty you can make your own frames to give the headboard a more polished look instead of having the clear hooks showing.

Another headboard idea is to purchase some plain canvas from Michaels or Hobby Town. Section off the canvas at different angles with some masking or painters tape and then sponge paint the sections different colors or one color. Once dry, remove the tape and the white of the canvas will blend in well with the new night stands you recycled. If you do not want to purchase canvas or can't afford to purchase canvas, search for a huge picture painted on canvas to use as a headboard.

Tip:

Explore limited possibilities

Chapter Eight

Fun Ideas for Children

We all know that children have too many toys for them to play with all at once. They love to pull out their toys but when it's time to clean up; this is where parents and grandparents are met with opposition (smile). Fear no more, here are some ideas that will have them wanting to clean up.

Idea One: Stuffed Animals

> Search for some old milk crates (4 or more), screw the bottom of the crates onto the wall side by. Get some plastic secure locks to secure the sides and top and bottom of the crates. Cut off the extra plastic after you have secured the locks tightly around the crates. These plastic locks can be found in the Dollar Tree, Wal-Mart or Family Dollar for around $1.00 or $1.50 for a pack of twenty. Stack the stuffed animals in the crates to free up some floor and bed space.

> Another option you can use for stuffed animal storage is the popup laundry bags. Use two of the laundry backs using thumbtacks or picture frame hooks to secure the popup laundry bags onto the wall.

The laundry bags can be stacked one on top of each other in the same direction or opposite direction. Or you can secure the laundry bags side by sides with the openings faced out. Once these bags are in place, the stuffed animals are ready to be put away.

Idea Two: Toy Box

Search for a bookcase with 3 to 4 shelves and remove the shelves. Turn the bookcase with the back on the floor and dump the toys in there. You can add some alphabet stickers on the bookshelf or cut out pictures from their coloring books and let the children tape their artwork to the recycled toy box.

The shelves that were removed from the bookcase can be used as floating shelves to stack books and smaller toys (i.e. Barbie dolls, tea sets, race cars, etc.). You can also personalize the toy box by spray painting. Allow your children to be creative with this toy box project. They will be excited about cleaning up their rooms.

Idea Three: Pillow Cases

Recycle old pillow cases as additional storage for toys by placing a pillow case on both sides of the room secured with something sturdy.

These pillow cases can be used for stuffed animals, dolls, or something light weight that will not rip the pillow case from the wall. The best part about this project is that you can use what you have at home if you can't find anything in a thrift store.

Idea Four: Sheets

Turn your old sheets into a hammock secured by plastic coat or wall hooks that stick to the wall. Make sure that the hooks are big enough so that you can tie the sheet at both ends to the hooks. Again, this is great for those bigger stuffed animals that take up too much floor space. Keep in mind that you want the hammock toy storage to be up high enough where the smaller child cannot climb into the hammock.

Tip:

Be creative when thinking of toy storage

Chapter Nine

Bedding and Furniture for Children

Children's bedding can be quite expensive especially with the different Disney characters on the market. Some of the best places to shop for bedding are at thrift or resale shops that specialize in children's clothing, furniture and accessories. The Goodwill or Salvation Army sell bedding for children which are sold as bed in a bag ensemble for around $15.00 up to $20.00 dollars. For me this is a little steep for children's bedding, that's why my first choice would be to search your local thrift or resale shops.

If you wanted to be creative and create your own theme below are a few ideas for boys and girls that you can try out along with the child (s) help and input. When children had a hand in fixing up their bedrooms they appreciate it more and are willing to keep their rooms clean.

Idea One: Hello Kitty Room Décor

Shop for a plain pink or white comforter or bedspread without any designs, this is important because you and your little one are going to be creative when creating this theme. Next, search for a Hello Kitty iron on sticker or decal from Wal-Mart or Target.

If you do not have any luck here for these decals and stickers, try Michaels Arts and Crafts store or any type of store that sell party favors such as Party City or the Party Store. Place the decal on the center of the comforter or bed spread using the distance of the pillow at the headboard as a guide to center your decal. If the comforter or bedspread comes with shams add a decal on the pillow sham.

For your curtains you can purchase or use some flat sheets in pink or white and get some tie backs. At the bottom of the sheets fold them over about 2 inches and hand stitch or sew them down leaving the sides open to insert your curtain rods that sell for about $2.00 bucks the most for a pack of two rods or you can check for them in the second hand store. For the best look whatever colors the comforter or bedspread is coordinate the sheets on the bed and for your curtains the same color.

Now for the nightstand you can purchase a side table from the thrift store, sand it down and paint it white and add some Hello Kitty stickers on the top of the side table. Also, search for a small lamp and switch out the lamp shade in either pink or white to coordinate with the theme. Be creative when decorating your little girls' bedroom. You want her bedroom to have the feel and look that you have purchased new bedding and furniture.

Idea Two: Ninja Turtle or Race Car Theme

These themes are so much fun to play around with by being creative. Get a solid color comforter of your choice, keeping the theme in mind. Example: Ninja Turtle theme color (s) green, yellow and red. Race Car theme color (s) red, black, white, blue or yellow. Check out the party store in your area for decals and banners. Locate a decal that can be ironed onto the center of the comforter and pillow sham. Banner (s) can be displayed on the walls. If you decide to go with the race car theme, search for the black and white checkered flags which can be displayed on both sides of the walls.

Some fun novelty items you can get for the Ninja Turtle theme are unlimited. There are so many pieces that you can use as wall decorations. The plastic swords can be displayed on the walls along with the helium balloons without the helium.

Also, tie some curly ribbon to the end of the balloons as additional decoration. If you can't find a ninja turtle decal and you are a good at sewing, use the ninja turtle shell from the costume and sew that onto the comforter. The different color ninja bandanas can be displayed with the names of the turtles across them. See example on next page.

For example, Leonardo's name glued on the blue bandana, Donatello's name glued on the purple bandana, Michelangelo's name glued on the orange bandana and Raphael's name glued on the red bandana. Make sure you have the correct names on the right colored bandanas.

Some of the décor ideas mentioned for Hello Kitty can be used for the Ninja Turtle and Race Car themes. (i.e. side tables with stickers etc).

Tip:

Stick with the color scheme of the theme you are going for

Chapter 10

DIY Home Decorations

In this chapter we will discuss some DIY ideas for vases and wall art. Most of these ideas I have created myself for my home. In fact, one of my ideas was so out of the box that a couple of friends copied it and gave me the credit (smile). You may have some ideas in mind of your own that you can share with your friends, but how would you know if you haven't ignited them. Let's began by uncovering your home decoration genius.

Idea One: Homemade Plant Decorations

Search in your back yard for some tree branches that are about an inch in thickness and the length of your arm. Remove all of the petals that are attached to the branches and smooth out the branches with a knife or some sand paper. Once the petals have been smoothed out you will lay the branches on some newspaper and spray paint the branches the color of your choice. You may have to spray paint the branches a couple of times, to make sure that the branches are fully covered. When I did this project I spray painted the branches black. The darker the branches the better the paint will stick.

For a finished look, make sure the spray paint has a gloss to it; this makes your creation look less of a DIY project.

These branches go well in a solid color or clear vase to sit on the coffee table or table of your choice. For vases that sit on the floor, the branches shall be the length of your legs or of your choice. The look you are going for is something out of a Home & Garden magazine.

Idea Two: Rock and Stones

Working with rocks and stones is such a fun project; I'm getting so excited just thinking about it. You can collect some rocks with a smooth look and within the same color family (i.e. brown, gray, white etc).

You may or may not want your rocks to be pointed or too chunky looking because the use of these rocks or stones determines the outcome of the project. Again, these rocks and stones can be found outside of your home. Once you have found your rocks, place them in some warm soapy water and let sit for about 20 to 30 minutes. Also, it doesn't hurt to re-rinse the rocks again to make sure all of the dirt has been removed.

Once the rocks and stones have been cleaned pat them dry with a paper towel. This step is important because now you are ready to spray some polyurethane on the rocks to give them a glossy look.

This project is more for the dining room table as the center piece. Use a glass vase which you can purchase from the Dollar Tree for $1.00 and place the stones in the bottom of the vase. You can place however many rocks you want, but I recommend about an inch to two inches high because this eliminate the rocks from overpowering the dining room table. When I mentioned that the rocks and stones should be flat and not chunky this is so the rocks and stones will not overpower the dining room table. Another idea for the rocks and stones, you can add some artificial flowers that compliment your dining room for a more formal look.

Idea Three: Crystal Clear Beads

The crystal clear beads I am referring to are bigger than marbles and can be found at any arts and crafts store but my focus is to get you the most for a buck. The Dollar Tree store sells these crystal clear beads in their arts and crafts section in a variety of colors packaged in a plastic bag.

If you choose to try this project, here is a clear indication that you have the right beads that I'm referring to. These beads have holes at both ends of them and there are some bigger pieces in the package shaped like diamonds. Once, you have located the colors you want you can place these marbles in the bottom of a vase and display in the room of your choice (i.e. living room, dining and bathroom).

Idea Four: Potpourri

Being creative using potpourri is the least expensive DIY project thus far. You can use any type of glassware that you can imagine. Oftentimes, I use potpourri in the bathroom or the living room. When using the potpourri in the bathroom, I used a small vase or a glass that can pass as a vase and pour a nice amount of potpourri into the glass. Once my potpourri is in the glass I place the glass on the tank of the toilet and wrap some artificial plants around the glass.

For the living room I will pour some potpourri into a bowl shaped plant holder filling to the top. The bowl can be placed on the fireplace mantel or placed on the coffee table. The potpourri filled to the top emits an aroma which fills the room when someone enters your home.

Potpourri is not expensive at all and it has been around for years. Some people prefer to leave the potpourri in the packaging it comes in as a decoration. Whatever your choice may be do know that it's affordable and can be purchased at the Dollar Tree for $1.00.

Idea Five: Artificial Plants

For the last few ideas, I will be referring to The Dollar Tree store to complete these easy affordable projects. As mentioned in the above idea, artificial plants can light up any room.

Here's an idea that I used in my half-bathroom that was one of my best creations thus far. I purchased some wicker wall sconces and inserted some artificial ivy plants in each one. The wall sconces were placed on the wall about 4 inches apart from each other with one sitting up higher than the other. The sconces were filled up and running over the top to give it a real effect. My guests thought that I had real plants in these sconces and they were stumped on how I was able to water the plants.

What I like about the artificial plants is the variety of plants that you can choose from. If you prefer the Chinese evergreen, Arrowhead or Boston ferns these are all available for $1.00 and under.

These artificial plants can be used on the top of your china cabinet or inside of the china cabinet and on top of your kitchen cabinets as a nice display.

Idea Six: China Cabinets

When using the artificial plants on top or inside of your china cabinet, be very creative. If you want to place your plants on top of the china cabinet, spread the plants out across the length of the china cabinet, you do not need to use a vase if you do not want to. The plants spread across draws the eye to the china cabinet from top to bottom. This gives your dining room more of an elegant look and a nice comfortable place to talk with your family or guest long after dinner has been served.

Displaying the artificial plants on the inside of your china cabinet is a nice conversation piece as well. When displaying on the bottom shelf of the china cabinet I think the best plants to use are evergreen plants because they have more flexibility. For example, let's say that you have a set of wine goblets in the center of your cabinet on the bottom shelf; you can wrap the evergreens around that center piece or have evergreen's lined up against the door and glass across the front or back of the goblets. This looks so elegant when the light is turned on inside of the china cabinet.

Idea Seven: Kitchen Cabinets

Most kitchen cabinets are high up against the ceiling and you can barely display things on top of them. When you do display things on top of your kitchen cabinets it is normally nice plates, knife set and/or the kitchen appliances in the boxes. Now I'm not saying that there is something wrong with this, because I have displayed the same things on top of my kitchen cabinets also. My goal is to give you a visual on other options.

Visualize this if your kitchen cabinets are over the kitchen sink use that space to display some artificial plants from corner to corner of that space. The artificial plants envelop the plate or glasses that you already had in place on display. It's your choice if you only want to place plants around the center piece or across the entire top cabinet from corner to corner.

Tip

Be creative and have fun while doing it

Conclusion

First of all I thank God for giving me this platform to share with you what I have learned over the years. It was a pleasure writing this eBook on "How to Shop for Less" for your reading pleasure. The ideas and tips I have shared with you are some of my personal experiences as well as my friends and family member experiences.

We all have hidden talents within us that need to be unleashed but we do not know where to start, so with that being said hopefully this eBook will help you in unleashing those talents on a budget. If you can add to or take any of these ideas I have shared then please pay it forward and share with your family and friends. Did you realize that sharing what you have learned is food to your soul, especially when you are sharing it with the ones you love and care about?

If this eBook has been helpful to you tell your loved ones how they can purchase their own copy for themselves or bless them with their copy available on Amazon.com. Also, keep an eye out for the paperback coming soon! Again, I thank you for embracing me as a new author and I'm grateful for your continued support.

www.ingramcontent.com/pod-product-compliance
Lightning Source LLC
Chambersburg PA
CBHW072026290526
45787CB00015B/2235